GROWING UP GREEN

GROWING UP GREEN

POEMS OF WONDER

FROM A HERITAGE
IN SCIENCE

ANNE ALEXANDER BINGHAM

191 Bank Street
Burlington Vermont 05401

Onion River Press
191 Bank Street
Burlington, VT 05401

Printed in the United States of America

ISBN: 978-1-949066-06-7

Cover Photo by Richard L. Bingham
Book Design: Marian Willmott, www.willmottstudios.com

"Growing Up Green" is dedicated to the
the many gifts that Anne gave to family and
friends. These poems were her response to life
events and they create a memoir for remem-
brance of her life.

-- Richard Bingham

Contents

III. East and West

FOREWORD

To read Anne Bingham's book of poems, Growing Up Green, is to be in the presence of a grounded soul, a person who knew herself and her world. At a time when many of us have been increasingly disconnected from our natural environment, it is such a pleasure to be with a person like Anne, a person at home with her surroundings.

Anne did not come to her love of the two places she called home – Colorado and Vermont – by accident. Her parents, biologists deeply engaged with the natural world, saw to it that she grew up feeling connected to nature--that she experienced nature firsthand and gained an intimate understanding and respect for the area's distinctive geography, climate, plants, and animals. Like the poet and environmentalist Wendall Berry, Anne came to realize that "if you don't know where you are, you don't know who you are."

In Anne's poems one feels her sense of place as she explores the relationship between herself and the places where she's lived. Claire Van Vliet, Vermont artist and printmaker, also liked mountains. And like Anne, she understood that "to conquer a mountain, you must stand on its highest peak. But to know it [that mountain], takes time." Anne's poems reflect her years of close observations—she was on a first name basis with all the flora and fauna. Many of her poems are set in the mountains she came to love, and readers, with Anne as their guide, easily share in all the sensual pleasures of being in the mountains – the smell of the 'early morning sage after a rain," the sounds of the "kinglet call," the rumbling of thunder, the feel of the rocks and tundra underfoot, the sight of meadows full of "forget-me-nots, alpine sunflowers . . . paintbrush, golden banner, columbine."

Closer to home, Anne witnessed the daily life-and-death dramas the played out around the backyard bird feeder. In the poem "Luck" she watches a Coopers Hawk, the "tiger of the bird world," silently stalk a nuthatch. The chickadees, squirrels, and doves, having sensed the presence of the hawk, have vacated the area. Suddenly, the hawk and the nuthatch are gone, the hawk searching for other prey from the treetops of Anne's woods and the nuthatch in hot pursuit of its own prey that inhabit the nooks of crevices of the trees' bark.

Always the teacher, Anne used her poetry as a vehicle to share her delight with science and her warmth and humor as a storyteller. Anne is the quintessential environmentalist. She understood just how important it is for all of us to maintain a fundamental connection to our natural surroundings. For it is in our basic connection to place that the survival of our human community and an inhabitable natural world depend. Like Anne, we crave a greater connection to the natural landscape, and yearn for this thing called "a sense of place." We all want to belong.

Paul Eschholz
Professor Emeritus of English, University of Vermont

I. GROWING UP GREEN IN THE WEST

GRASSHOPPERS

Picture an open field with tall grasses, and here and there spots of yellow, lavender and red flowers of the high plains in Colorado. Just beyond the field the ground rises sharply, the beginning of the foothills of the Rocky Mountains. As these hills continue to gain altitude they are covered with a scattered growth of ponderosa pine. Looking up, flat slabs of red sandstone jutting from the higher hills will grab your attention. These huge formations-The Flatirons-form the unique backdrop for a quiet college town. Growth and reputation will come later.

Back to the field: A child enters, perhaps seven or eight years old. She moves deliberately, sweeping an insect net back and forth through the grass in front of her. Finally stopping, she gathers the net tight near the opening and runs back through the field to a tall man on his knees in the grass. Beside him is a similar net and several glass jars with fat cork stoppers. Together they open her net and peer in, carefully pulling out grasshoppers one at a time. She has learned to hold the hopper gently with fore-finger and thumb across the thorax. The current captive scrambles helplessly with its strong back legs unable to gain purchase for a leap. Turning its head it spits "tobacco" on her finger which she will absent-mindedly wipe later on her shorts. Right now they are occupied with moving the captive into a jar. The cork stopper has been hollowed out to allow the insertion of cyanide crystals covered by blotting paper held in place by pins driven into the cork. She has learned to handle the jar with care and respect, but not fear.

Are you concerned about the innocent victim? Please understand that this is science. The grasshopper is not fish bait, but rather a tool of research to better understand ecology and evolution in relation to mountain environments. The child is myself and my childhood was full of moments like this: the man, my father, professor of biology at the University of Colorado. And the research reverberates to this day as ecologists revisit his research sites at various altitudes to better understand the effects of global warming.

IMAGES OF THE WEST

I feel the West in my feet:
    Memory of trails winding up mountains,
    Pressure of rocks searched by sight
        tested by feet,
    A bridge to walk across mountain streams.

The West returns to me in scents:
    Early morning sage after a rain,
    Dry pine needles,
    Moist stream banks.

My chest expands, heart opens up,
    Echoes the endless sky
    Surrounding the high dessert.

The West sounds in my ears:
    The kinglet call,
    The eagle cry,
    The tumbling stream,
    And rumbling thunder.

In the West I taste the sweet afternoon rain:
    My skin is caressed by the soft mountain breeze,
    My mind dwells in memory and reflection of
    Mountains covered with lodgepole pines,
        Spruce, fir, and golden aspen.

High in the West:
    Tundra crunches under my feet,
    Bright July miniatures,
        Forget-me-nots, alpine sunflower,
    Flowers of the montane,

Paintbrush, golden banner, columbine,
Rivers flow from snowmelt - east or west
And on high plateau, sculpted stone
Above scattered cattle
Nature and culture now dance together.

THE VISIT

I'd seen the marks
on an aspen tree down by the creek
the lines above my head cut through white bark
                    Cleanly

But neither of us was prepared to meet, I think
in the heat of that lazy afternoon
as I stepped onto the cabin porch
preparing to throw out
                    dishwater

What was his errand, or hers
up on the hillside
twenty feet away

I grasped my pan of soapy water
she stared down at me
curious perhaps, unafraid certainly

I, on the other hand,
was glad to have the cabin
at my back

Then she loped up the hill
twigs crackling
and I moved, too
put down the dishpan, ran for the camera
            proof certain of my visitor

Later I found a tangled bit of
brown fur caught in
pine bark

it could have been moss

Only that
    the image in my head
        unemptied dishwater
           and unexposed film.

LONGS PEAK COLORADO

We climbed all day, slept and climbed again,
No footprints now as feet touch rock and rock,
The wind our adversary.

Standing I swing full turn, and see all stone
Swept clean with blue above, this mountain
Solid under me was once fluid, cooled and hardened.

What great power thrust her up, twisted, buckled
And scattered, one side sliced as with a knife,
We peer down that cut.

Specks below shift - climbers, their ropes not visible
On that Face thrust up recently as mountains go
We are all bitten by the wind.

The mountain crumbles slowly, invisibly
Soil building lichens, midget plants cling to granite
And create cracks to be filled with expanding ice.

Grasses grow there, perhaps a columbine or tree seed.
Plants tear down mountains if you can wait
A hundred, hundred thousand years or so.

SPRING COMES TO THE GUNNISON VALLEY

On a far hill
The aspen are leafmg out.
What was gray smoke of bare branches
Is now a creeping green.

Through the sagebrush
Spring is creeping.
Splotches of red –
Indian Paintbrush appear,
And small pink blossoms in the cactus.

Out of the sky,
A flash of blue.
Bluebirds have arrived,
An Oriole sings.

Even the ants
Are busy.
A bumble bee
Is in the current bush.

My granddaughter
Walks bare footed
In the grass,
Leaps and skips like a young calf.

Welcome Spring!

FLEXIBLE FLYER

The name can still be read
marching down the center wooden slat
among patches of red paint
rusted runners lean against the
attic wall, ready
pull rope listless
          waiting

Early morning after
the snow
we shout across
the street
a dozen kids

We post a lookout at the
bottom of the block
trudge to the top
not much traffic on Fourteenth Street as it
pitches down from Baseline Road

Already the rope freezes
to knit mittens as
we wait our turn
breath steaming
we assess the hill

Then run
flop down on your belly and
give a mighty push with both hands

Picking up speed
past the vacant lot on the corner

past Billy Smith's house
past the music teacher sweeping her steps
flying

With no car in sight
you might keep going
past the lookout
       another block

Or – car coming
       steer sharp right
       hit the curb with a soft thud

Hard balls of snow cling
to wool snow pants as
you take your turn as lookout

Morning after the storm

TWENTY BELOW

Accordion pleats of the West Elk Wilderness
have gathered snow this
clean harsh morning
diamond crystals frost the valley
Carbon Peak a bold white pyramid
against
expansive blue

While snug against the backyard shed
curled in a circle of snow
a doe studies the landscape
slowly chewing
ears twitch
taking in the silence
a pane of glass between us

How long would I survive
living on the other side
I would need layers from the skin out
two or three on my legs
sweaters, parka, hat, mittens
(at least two pairs),
boots and many socks
What do the Himalayan climbers wear?

And what about inner warmth
something to fuel my metabolism
gray leaves of sagebrush would not
do the job for me

My hands circle a mug of hot tea
the scent of toast reaches my nose

a jar of marmalade is on the table
yet I stay and shiver by the window
caught up in the tension between
death and beauty
outside the pane

VERA

Came as a bride to this cabin
under the Continental Divide
Tom worked at the
Smuggler Mine
Moon Gulch their address

Fall-they'd drive the wagon
down the canyon, twenty-five miles
spend the night at the
old Boulderado Hotel
load up potatoes, onions, cabbage
       winter fodder

Saturday night in winter
walk ten miles for a dance
dance all night

When the dance hall
closed for good
Tom brought home
the floor boards
built a nice long room across
the front of the cabin
making three

I sit on Vera's porch now
a squirrel is burying a pine cone
over by the barn
his winter fodder--seed saved
      like a memory

Like Vera who sits beside me as

the dead often do
their stories run our lives backward
to even before our time
and they linger on the sidelines
watching
lending their courage

INDIAN

Brown–boy

      dancing

Head–back

      head–down

Toe–heel

      a–round

A–round

      circle

        a–round

Drum–beat

      makes–him

      proud

Tonight he is an Indian boy

Tomorrow he goes to school

Acts white

      reads white

      lives white

But tonight he is Indian

      Dancing to the drum beat

Proud!

BEGINNINGS IN SCIENCE -1917

Found my father's Nature Diary and opening the pages

Was opening the life of a sixteen year old who roamed the
Missouri River Valley

Foretelling the scientist he would become, he didn't know that he
was also to be my father

A sixteen year old like and unlike other boys, the panorama of
nature fascinated him

Meticulous drawing of a fossil nautilus embedded in a piece of
Niagara limestone

Price list from the Marine Biological Laboratory: "The classifica-
tion of marine animals will help me a great deal in my work."

"Finished the text of 'Five Common Species of the Genus
Murex, about 1000 words in all."

Request for membership in the Kansas City Kansas Society of
Natural Science

Caught a number of insects: Lepidoptera, Orthoptera, Hemiptera
and increased bird list from 42 to 45: Dickcissel, Nighthawk, Blue
Grosbeak

"Started my vacation off splendidly by building a lean-to in the
willows about 3 miles from home A fine place for studying birds
along the bank of the Missouri River

continued

Working with a friend we saw several large butterflies and orthoptera are abundant

Ordered from Ward's Natural Science Establishment a couple of trilobites, a set of dissecting instruments, 3 shells, an 80 page catalogue of Lepidoptera, cost $2.00

Counted twelve species of trees in one block from home to school as follows ....

MEASURING THE TREES, COLORADO 2002

I put my arms around the tree, cheek against rough bark.
Fingers do not meet on the other side
    no matter how I press my body-to the sturdy trunk.

I break off a lump of gold and sniff it closely–hardened sap
Perhaps an insect or a woodpecker broke through the bark
    and bled the tree here.

My searching fingers find a recent wound, bleeding stickiness
It will heal.
More amber drops will form here.

Avoiding stickiness, I reach around the trunk one more time.
I am measuring the trees
Trying to remember them sixty years ago.

Bark flakes as I tip my head,
sight up along an arrow straight trunk.

Stiffly erect trees such as this–younger though–
once held in place the buffalo robes of tepee covers.
Lodgepole Pine they were and are called still.

Viewed through needles and a whorl of branches, the
sky is not the azure of even recent memory.
The spine of the tree rises instead
to smoke softened turquoise.

Trees are burning all over the west
acres and acres of forest

continued

I try to envision the size of these trees sixty years ago
when I first knew them.
Growth so slow, over their lifetime
my lifetime

What size this tree when a ten year old passed by,
gathering rocks and pinecones?

Pinecones
I look among dry needles where trunk enters soil,
becomes root.
There are a few cones, but over my head
they crowd the branches
clinging, waiting for heat to open them,
to rain down seeds.

Fire and the trees have made mutual accommodation.
Fire and the trees have lived together longer
than my friendship with this particular tree.

This fact pushes to enter my thinking, my logic,
as I try to assess the risk to these mature lodgepoles
and to the tiny cabin in their midst
the risk this year when the west is burning.

Flaking bark, needles, cones,
strong trunk, deep roots
A pine at its maturity
wounded
healed

Again I place my cheek against the trunk
My arms measure its girth
Knowing now our shared mortality

WHEN YOUR GRANDPARENTS DIED

I did not share my grief with you

I cried alone, and

Wept at night when

Your father could enfold me.

Sobs shook me then,

Wrenching, tearing.

Perhaps you heard them

Alone in your rooms.

I did not share my grief with you,

A gift I should have given

Had I the strength.

My parents were your good friends too.

Did you also grieve alone,

Did you shed tears like me?

Would I had let you cling to me and cry,

I did not know shared grief to be a gift.

Another time of grief will come dear ones,

Meanwhile forgive me for this unsharing.

THE VERY MISCHIEF

Her name was Mischief–
light-hearted, affectionate
and, yes, mischievous.
Greeting with a
wriggling whole-body welcome,
no languid tail wagging.
She lived her name.

They arrived together,
sister and brother,
tumbling puppies who
needed a loving home–
food, fence, exercise.

With a coat dense and comfy,
ready for winter,
she slept in the cold.
While her brother might curl up
warm, indoors.

On a run,
flying over the ground
she was exuberant
summer or winter,
mountain path or ski trail.
What joy!

Ringleader–
If there was an opportunity to
escape,
ignore her name,
get into trouble,

she led the way.

Who pulled the sled?
Brother and sister in harness
together,
yet without her it would not fly
over the frozen ground.

So much our canine companions
teach us about love and caring.
Friend,
          comforter,
                    model of feminist independence,

We miss you LOKI!

LEARNING TO LIVE TOGETHER

On our Honeymoon–
    Forgot his toothbrush and said,
    "Sharing a toothbrush is a
       Sign of true love."

    Looked at his breakfast,
    A perfectly fried egg,
       Toast and jam.

    Said – "But I always have two."

CARESS

The caressing breeze

Soft, dry, gentle

Like my mother

Brushing back

The hair on my forehead

Comfort

DOGSLED

The two dogs pull willingly,
    Old friends
Brother and sister.

On the back my granddaughter
    Stands on the runners
Her head not much above the sled back.

Her mother runs along the side
    As they move through
A blue and white world -
    Her world.

Winter child of snow loving parents -
    Joyful!

II. IN THE EAST

NAMES

I grew up catching grasshoppers, but that wasn't the only con-
sequence- privilege really- of having two parents who were
biologists. There were trips out onto the plains to visit reservoirs
where water birds gathered during migration- ducks, sandpip-
ers, and the elegant avocet unmistakable with its stilt legs, long
upturned bill and cinnamon head and neck. My father took me
to visit a heron rookery where great blue herons created their
messy nests from twigs and branches high in a grove of cotton-
wood trees. Driving on the plains we always kept an eye out for
burrowing owls, perched on the barbed wire fences. Now endan-
gered, these long-legged small owls lived in unused prairie dog
burrows.

The names of living things were important in my family along
with how to identify them so you could recognize their faces
when you met again: faces of Indian paintbrush, limber pine,
grey headed junco, and the pika. Pikas are wonderful small ro-
dents, most closely related to rabbits. They live among the rock
scree near and above timberline. This little creature spends the
summer months making hay, spreading grass on the rocks to dry
and store for winter fodder.

Back to names: I've heard non-scientists make fun of this pre-
occupation with identifying and naming plants or birds. The
suggestion is that with all this detailed inspection and reference
to field guides you somehow miss out on the beauty of nature.
They couldn't be more mistaken. What a pleasure to walk along a
stream and find your friend the pink shooting star, or grab a

continued

prickly branch and know immediately"spruce, not fir." You would never imagine you could enjoy your human friends if you ignored or never learned their names.

My mother was particularly concerned with teaching those characteristics of identity and the corresponding names. She made up rhymes to help learn trees. All I remember of them now is to look for "little mouse ears" to identify the cones of Douglas Fir. She didn't insist on scientific names, but did use them herself quite a lot. There was a reason. An "Indian Paintbrush" may be quite a different flower in New England than in the West, but a scientific name identifies the plant worldwide. For those in the know it also gives some clues about near relatives.

MOUNTAIN TOWN

Early morning
The little league field
Is mist filled
With crows strutting

Yesterday
The burnished sun beat
Down on kids in uniforms
Home runs shouted

Now, checkered in dawn
Silent crows
Where are their voices ?
Swagger among the ghost skirted clouds

EARLY MORNING

Early morning creeps in through straight trunks and leaf lattices
    Pools of gold replace the grey
The old pole fence leans lakeward and across the water
    I hear a rooster crow and birds stir above my head.

Our old dog has had an early morning amble
    I sit outside the tent while she noses her blind way
I get her water from the thermos, she laps
    And I heat coffee for myself.

    My sleeping bag was warm
        But now the day's promise
    Creeps in with the gold and I am
        Tugged out by an old dog.

THE WARMING EARTH

I feel the stirring underneath
As rootlets reach for sustenance
Upward through the dark wet tunnels
Preparing to behold the light and know new worlds.

Beside me and above, fat buds
Are swelling hour by hour
Preparing for the moment of unfolding
Finger, palm leaf and flower to reach, grasp and feel.

The moment is near
For a bursting forth and
Life will have its way. The process
Cannot be stopped now, it only waits one sunny day.

SWAMP

The swamp spreads pewter surface to a pewter sky
Pierced only by grass blades, and on slender single limb
A heron hunched and pewter too, unmoving.

From horizon's orange coals a red ball rises
The grey neck stretches skyward and another leg
Slowly moves forward, long toes slipping through the water.

The stalking hunter strikes stabbing the water
And brings up a splashing, flapping breakfast.
I wish the sun could wake me to such concentrated purpose
As I contemplate the day over a warm cup of coffee.

ISAAC

Lies down beside me

    Cold tummy on the sun warmed dock

He eyes me with two-year old caution

    Then looks down between the boards

He stares, with eye to crack to watch

    The water in the shade beneath

"Oh woggy!" he says to crayfish

    Crawling among the stones, "Fishy!"

Grown-ups sitting on the beach

    Watch the trees, the lake, the splashing children

An hour passes while Isaac has discovered

    A world beneath that crack

"Oh woggy!" "Oh fishy!"

THE FREEZING

The lake is still this morning
no white caps travel north to south
no ripples circle out from a tossed stone
February
it will remain like this I think
although in this strange winter
it has frozen and opened three times
proof of climate change we think.

Can the heart's climate change?
the soul freeze?
I cannot seem to decide today
what to do next
my hand stops the cup in mid-air as
I stare out the window.

An hour ago my friend called
her husband died last night
went to sleep, she said, and didn't wake
she got up, walked the dog
then returned to the bedroom and
tried to rouse him from the pillow.

How often I have reached across
the space between the sheets
to place a hand against your back
to find it warm
and sink back into safety.

SNOWSHOES

Silence- I stop and hug it to me
Our woods are not far from the highway
But padded and insulated with snow
There are moments of quiet.
A chickadee breaks the silence
And calls members of its flock.

I move away from the house
Deeper into the woods
Some days the magic is tracks
Our fox winds through his territory
Mostly unseen except for a line of paw prints
One day we watched him catch a mouse
Pounce, pounce, catlike.

Squirrels have created their own highway
Headed directly for our birdfeeder
Mouse track stitch the fence to a fallen tree
Each tree trunk today has a long
White stripe up its south side
That marks the direction of the storm.

Overnight all will change
Ice crystals will lose their interlocking points
And slump together
Tomorrow the magic will be different
What will I find on my big feet?

POETRY IN THE MIDST OF DISSONANCE

A mountain of debris sits
     between the garden and
         the ash tree
white sheetrock
     pink insulation
         splintered floorboards with nails sticking
out
consequence of a burst pipe.

The snow is gone
     for the time being.

A line of green is winter hyacinths,
     while beyond the split rail fence
         and brown-gold forest floor
           of oak and maple
a chickadee is singing.

MORNINGS

Mornings I read poetry, sipping tea

Sometimes I read one poem after another

Sometimes one catches me and I stop there

Memories lift softly as mist from a pond

Old friends gather, children leap and cry

I close the book and move into my new day

Enabled to embrace what opens before me.

WAVES ON OUR BEACH

Waves make lacy soft ruffles on our rocky beach

    Cush sh sh sh, Cushshshshsh

Foam submerges grey shale, flattens, flows back

    Cush sh sh sh, Cushshshshsh

Waves make lace again, petticoats upon the beach

    Cush sh sh sh, Cushshshshsh

Air and water soon gone, sucked back into the lake

    Cush sh sh sh, Cushshshshsh

Lacy petticoats fanned out to dry upon the stones

    Cush sh sh sh, Cushshshshsh

Now there're gone- Woossh!- Now they come again

    Cush sh sh sh, Cushshshshsh

BARE VERMONT JANUARY

Is this winter, this hard, dull ground of grey and brown?

    Where are the blue shadows I remember,

Pastel sunsets of mauve and pink on a snowy hill?

    Where are the skiers from New York and Massachusetts

Car tops ridged with poles, curved ski tips, fiberglass and wood?

    No lone Nordic skier moves outside my window

Swinging legs and arms with each glide forward, poles in rhythm.

    No roar of snow plow shakes the ground

leaving a ridge of snow across my driveway to be shoveled

    In a cold early morning exercise.

Snow will come, we say, next month as we cross the hard grey

brown.

VERMONT APRIL

The bare branches
speak to me
twisted cherry
shaggy bark of hickory
massive oak
the erect trunks of maple dividing upward

I know their time of nourishment
is coming
botanic blood coursing upward
a canopy of leaves
feeding, breathing

But—I love the gift of light their
dormancy allows
the long view
of forest floor
branches opening to me
        the life of birds
        feeding, pairing
        visible sky, sun, air

The earth is resting still
eyes open
yet curled beneath the blanket
ready to wake slowly
stretch
taking time to get on with
the frantic work ahead
all this
        growth and sex
        making seeds, hatching fledglings

a continued need to reproduce
to insure the forest life persists
in the short months
between now and next
winter's rest

LUCK

Hawk
Coopers Hawk–tiger
of the bird world
clutches a fallen log
outside my window
just beyond the bird feeder

Two eyes burn
divided by a razor beak
while wind lifts feathers softly
on a gray-orange breast
contradicting the military posture
tail a striped flag

On the other side
of the bird feeder
hidden like a leaf caught in the perch
a nuthatch hangs
upside down
motionless

Only the head of the hawk moves
turning
turning
talons making channels in
the old hickory

my breath stops
minutes pass
I think to dash out the door
dispersing both birds
but instead I wait

frozen on my side of the window

The smaller bird
waits and wins
the hawk lifts off
and veering between branches
disappears
in silence

Minutes pass
I slowly let my breath out
Nothing stirs
no whirring chickadee wings
no acrobatic squirrels raid the feeder
no doves harvest dropped seed on the ground

finally the nuthatch shakes a wing
looks up
more minutes
then
both are gone

The hawk somewhere searching
with its burning eye
from the treetops of my woods

The nuthatch
its nasal note rising
spirals down a trunk
searching somewhere under oak or maple bark
for its hidden prey

So the fox creeps and pounces

continued

the mouse runs
the osprey dives and grasps the gleaming fish
that has been seeking small fry of the lake

My human insight would like to bestow
on the small bird
wisdom, planning, foresight and memory
but of course it wasn't these
only instinct
and luck
especially luck

SUMMER COTTAGE

An ancient canning jar
sits on the shelf
crammed with cherry pits.
Someone attached a sign
"Guess how many."

Remember:
sitting in the shade
sheltered from the beating sun
sticky with cherry juice
prying out the pits with a half-opened hairpin
sucking the sour-sweet fruit
and watching the sailboats on the water
out beyond the cedars?

On the shelf beside the cherry pits
a chipped cup and saucer
saved from great-grandmother.
How many cups of tea here
mine with milk and sugar?

A wall of souvenir photos
summon many summers:
small grandson on a tractor with grandpa
beside it a photo of a new tractor
grown grandson driving
generations mixed and matched
in a collage of kin

Pictures on the wall reflect

continued

the lake outside the windows:
in one a braided beauty, twelve years old
waves from the dock
next a three year old leaps with a splash
caught by those same arms
now grown
mother

And that proud photo of grandpa
with a flat of raspberries
enough raspberries to satisfy
anyone's passion
and tomatoes
globes of big boy and beefsteak
heaped in the wheelbarrow

He didn't grow corn
not to compete with the raccoons
so we watched the farm stands
bought corn the day it appeared
had to be picked that morning

Later the children carried a dishpan into the woods
filled with empty corncobs pooled in butter
and perhaps clamshells, apple cores, pea pods
We said, "Go feed the skunks."
If it was dusk the task was fraught with danger
and they scurried back
watching over their shoulders
leaping rocks and roots

I can't remember the prize for
guessing how many cherry pits,
or when we got the new tractor
what summer the sailboat arrived

Only the long family table
under the sky
differences forgotten
anger shelved and sorrow set aside
though politics and religion were a sore topic
even the vicissitudes of weather are
erased from memory

Only the long family table
the lake and the sky

THE WORD IS OUT

The deer are eating my hostas.
The word is out.
There's a great garden salad to be had
at 30 Featherbed Lane or
whatever address a deer might use

How do they know?
A doe discovers a delicacy
in the dead of night.
Does she keep it to herself
or invite her friends for
a feast under the stars?

I am blind to the trespass
and if I saw her I might melt.
As it is we apply pepper spray
again and again
after the rain.

———————————

One day in June
we have another visitor.
I wouldn't call it trespass this time.
Like flitting yellow lilies
the swallowtails appear
blossoms on the wing.

The lilac is in bloom.
The word is out
promise of sweet nectar
particularly appealing for this species

and they cover the pale purple blossoms
with constant bright motion
until petals begin to drop
and as suddenly as they came
they are gone.

How does the word get out?
How do these visitors know
to find their culinary delights
where we live in the woods?
What telegraph travels through the air
in a language we do not share?

CONTENTMENT

The kids call
to check on us
to invite us to
get out of winter
come visit.

They know winter is long
the yard is full of snow and ice,
and I made the mistake of asking
what's blooming in Salem, Oregon
where something blooms
every month of the year?

So the invitation came.
How can we convince them
we're fme
especially since we have nothing
exciting to report?

They should see the house
clutter, like it hasn't been
since they were little
all my toys
    photo albums
    craft projects
    cook books
    half-written poems
and books
    Dad's daily Times.

How can we convince them
of our contentment

born of fifty-seven years as best friends?

Then, the nearer ones
grown-up kids from Massachusetts
plan a visit
assuring us they "need to get away"
to see the lake iced over
and we wonder
    are they checking up on us?
    do they wonder
how we are managing?

An article in the newspaper tells
fifty-year olds how to talk to their
aging parents.
Did they read this?

We are harsh.
We say: We'd love to see you
    but:
Don't come if you are driving
that old undependable car.
We can't rescue you.
And don't come if there is a storm.
And above all don't come if
    you are sick.
We love you
    but not your germs.

Crotchety, comfortable, content
We're fine.
We love you.
Phone often!
And come when the sun is shining.

THE OLD LOG

The old log –

    Once a sentinel shagbark hickory

Now a jungle gym for chipmunks

    They run through its hollow core.

What a good way to end a life –

    A playground for chipmunks.

MY BOOKS

I turn down the page comers

    Of my books –

An act of familiarity

    And ownership.

Now I know that it is

    About love.

When I'm gone

    You can know me

By what I returned to

    Again and again.

CREATION

Everywhere we create:
    The garden arrangement
What we plant next to
    That giant hosta
Where to place the
    The miniature iris.

Waking at night to create
    A lesson plan for
That one child who can't
    Get it - borrowing
And carrying - how to
    Present it differently
With blocks
    With poker chips.

Artists creating, revising;
    Making a marriage,
A home, a loaf of bread
    With cheese and
Sundried tomatoes.

Each one of us
    An artist,
Creating our life,
    Running, skipping,
Together or apart.

III. EAST AND WEST

THE STUDY

Mother was an avid gardener, often found working in her rock garden in the early morning hours, chatting with neighbors who walked by in front of our house. She collected rock garden plants and exchanged seeds that she kept in little packets in the refrigerator. She had a compost pile before anyone else I knew did such a thing, and spoke knowingly about the value of egg shells and coffee grounds in the making of rich soil.

Our refrigerator had yet another use besides food storage. Because my father knew how to mount birds and make up bird skins, people would sometimes give him dead birds that they found. If the bird was in good condition and perhaps not in the collection of the Biology Department, it would go in the refrigerator to be preserved until Dad could work on it.

My father's study contained many fascinations: the globe and atlas which took me to other worlds, a wall of books, many of them fat with pictures of birds, animals and insects. Also, most interesting of all, the book with pictures of babies growing inside their mother's bodies. Sitting on the maroon carpet I could be content among these books for a long time. A picture of Charles Darwin with a long white beard (no men I knew had beards) looked gently down from the wall above the desk.

Sometimes the door to the study was closed. Then my father was grading papers from his biology classes, working on a lec

continued

ture, or writing a paper or a book. I was always to knock and then only if I was quite sure it was very important to see him. My mother impressed me with this rule, and I always followed it. Usually I was graciously invited in, my father stooping slightly to bring his tall frame closer to me.

EAST AND WEST

What is this July jungle?

The openings I left in May are filled with green

    Creeping wild grape, osier and buckthorn,

Filling the understory space, obscuring the shape of the land.

I miss the hills and cliffs of high desert land

    Starkly sculpted:

The bones of the land made visible.

What is it makes the heart cling to a spare

    And bare landscape,

And the spirit celebrate the long view?

Nurtured under that vast sky, who paced those

    Rocky trails, inhaled the sage brush fragrance

And woke to the meadowlark song:

I do not find comfort in so much green.

WINTER'S GIFT

The world is stark and white tonight
    as muffled I go in the soft snow.
The air I breathe is sharp and clean
    the world is still.
It almost takes my breath away
    to reach the tree upon that hill
To stand alone, and accept
    the dare of winter.

MAGIC*

There's magic in the winter time,

And magic in the spring,

For if there isn't magic, here

There can't be anything.

What makes the rain turn into snow?

What makes it fall at all?

Why do the flowers bloom in May?

Why do the trees grow tall?

You see there must be magic,

It must be everywhere,

It must be in the sunshine,

That's shining on your hair.

*This is a poem Anne wrote in highschool in Boulder, Colorado, published in a regional collection of student poetry probably in 1946 or 47.

GREEN THUMB

I found her in the garden today

Working the Brownian-D.Vigna soil *

Stirring new life into the dirt

With her love for the earth.

I saw her like a divine Creator

And how her soul, like her garden

Is nursed by an evergreen thumb

In the fresh clear goodness of the open air.

* Botanists: Domenico Vigna (d .1647-ltaly) and
Robert Brown (d. 1858-Scotland)

INSOMNIA

Curled up with my book
Mug of warm milk
Not sleeping

My face reflected back
From un-curtained windows,
The house alone in the woods

I feel safe because I
Know you are there in
The next room
Dreaming

I can feel you breathing
Through the wall

When you are not here
My face stares back
From the black, blank windows

And I wonder who/what is on
The other side
Staring back at me, alone

But tonight
I feel you breathing
Through the wall

A THREE-FOR-ALL

LONG WINTER

There was an old crow from Champlain

Who said this is really a pain

The lake is all ice, my life's lost its spice

I think I'll fly over to Spain

HOUSE WARMING

A man that I knew built a house

In the country along with his spouse

When they moved in the neighbors came by:

Three chipmunks, two squirrels, and a mouse.

GARDENING

Your yellow marigolds shouted

While my pale pink petunias wept in the rain

Why didn't I plant marigolds?

THIS CHILD

Around the pond she runs ahead

Totters really and I hold my breath

This child, this gem divergent from

What is and what might have been

A child who grows taller

Yet doesn't grow or learns

So slowly, it seems so

Safe with Daddy near

Her guardian year by year.

FRAGMENTS

The fragments of my life float on a muddy river

It is spring and the water boils and churns

Fragments bob and spin away, sometimes

Come together, most often not

Spinning they rush along

The current eddies and I am restless.

STROKE

The loom grows dusty, the piano silent
She sits against heaped pillows, right hand reaches
Lifts the left to hide it beneath the sheet
The right foot kicks the left to a new position.

Let go the talent that moves toward design
As yarn in shuttle moves and feet shift pedals
To change warp and weft.
No longer count the measures in an etude's flow
While hands interpret the composers mind
In the play of ear, hand, and brain.

Yet she teases and creates a halting banter
Wrapping her tongue carefully around each word.
"You're sending me to stay right over the San Andreas fault
And I can't even walk." She smiles a crooked smile,
The ambulance moves out on the road to San Francisco.

Every member of the family left behind
Follow her with special hopes for rehabilitation.
The younger son of five says, "The new hospital
Will teach my mother how to smile again like this."
Hopes of the ten year old lie hidden.
When his father on return shows how the therapist
Taught mother to turn over
I read dismay in his restlessness.

And what of the husband-father? Can he hope?
Or shaken through the fog of grief – accept
And begin to prepare the house for wheelchair widths,
Examine the hall for space to turn
And remove the front door step.

IT IS ENOUGH *

To know that the atoms
of my body
will remain.

To think of them rising
through the roots of a great oak
to live in
leaves, branches, twigs.

Perhaps to feed the
crimson peony
the blue iris
the broccoli,

Or rest on water
freeze and thaw
with the seasons.

Some atoms might become a
bit of fluff on the wing
of a chickadee
to feel the breeze
know the support of air.

And some might drift
up and up into space,
star dust returning from
whence it came.

It is enough to know that
as long as there is a universe
I am a part of it.

*Read by Garrison Keillor on the PBS "The Writer's Almanac,"
January 22, 2014

DARK WINGS

Spring didn't come

last year.

I – strapped down

in my coffin

felt the dark birds hovering.

Their stinking breath

made me curl beneath my bonds,

cover my head.

Overcome by darkness

I could not weep.

But spring comes now,

Soft and tenuous,

Ready at any moment

to retreat.

Some days the dark wings hover,

Ice enters my bones.

Then the dark retreats.

Light enters my world.

The green comes.

Is it possible to trust the spring?

SPRING BIRTHING

I walked today in
    Rain
Feet sinking in sod

Saw trees blurred by
    A curtain of wet drops
Slick stones with shining faces

I have known other labors
    Wet, prolonged as this
And greeted shining faces

Through vision
    Blurred
By perspiration drops

MARGARET

She is with us
on any forest trail we walk
She preserved and created trails
    sweated, hauled branches, rolled boulders
    tenting in the deep woods
    living simply
She is there on the trail

She is with us
across this great land
where she hiked the
    mountains and the deserts
    rafted the Colorado River
    ocean to ocean
and beyond
She didn't stop there
    England
    Italy
    Africa
She is there as we open to diverse natural spaces

She is with us
in a house on the mountain top
when we gather on a wide porch
overlooking the Appalachian Trail
or settle comfortably on a chaise
where we can stare down steep slopes
to the lake far below
    the logs
    the stairs

continued

the very kitchen
remind us of her
She is here in this house

She is with us
in the quilts
creative, inventive, unique
Her love of the earth and its creatures are
there, in the design
    beach and sandpipers
    deer, owl, bear
She is there

She is with us
in lives
lives of children she touched
kids struggling to read
learning to swim
friends with whom she worked and hiked
a loving family
    children, grandchildren
    nieces and nephews
    brothers and sisters
She is there as we remember her and live out her example

She didn't just visit this earth
She lived it
Loved its wildness
    woods, water, animals, birds
taking the world in her arms
She is with us now in that world
    woods, water, animals, birds, human friends
Always

MARKET AT VERETTES

At dawn they begin to arrive
    Carrying what they have to sell or trade

Slender, erect women, skirts swinging
    On their heads are
        heavy baskets of produce
            bright plastic tubs piled with neatly folded
clothing
        bundles of firewood
           a five gallon bucket of water
      a large pot with a stand for cooking

As each arrives at her own spot in the market
    The women help each other lower their loads

A man helps his wife
    One arrives with his own load of firewood
        another makes his way down the narrow path
    between stalls
           bent double
    His gray head barely visible above the heavy bag of
corn
        across his shoulders

Someone leads a donkey
    Charcoal heaped in woven bags hanging down each
    side
Another donkey is rendered invisible under a burden of
sugarcane

A pig arrives in a tap-tap

continued

Quite like the one that transported us to Verettes this morning
    a small pick-up bouncing over the rocks

They spread their merchandise
    Sneakers and flip-flops heaped on a table
        baskets of produce
    Bright fabrics hung on horizontal poles
        a small mat heaped with machetes
    Sweet potatoes in neat piles
        each enough for a meal?

And buyers arrive with their small bundle
    Of the Haitian currency called gourds
        or with something to trade
    They arrive by
        bicycle
        riding a donkey
        one on a motorcycle but mostly on foot

Blaring horns of tap-taps shout continually just outside the market
    Blending with the constant murmur of Creole
        Bonjou!
        Konbyen (How much)?
        M pa vle li (I don't want it)!
    And the bargaining begins

We move into the bustle
    Make our way down a narrow path
        jumping aside for a load of produce in a wheelbarrow
    Skirting a dog fight near the cooking pots
        barely avoiding putting our toes in the hot coals
    Reluctantly refusing a beggar
        M regrete (I'm sorry)
Smoke from the fires
    Heat from the sun

A narrow path leads between heaps of clothing
    On mats
    On tables
    A tangle of color
        skirts
        blouses
        long pants
        shorts
    Along the front of another stall on an overhead pole
        bras panties scarves

Most women wear a scarf over the forehead
    Tied behind
    Only a few have hats
Many men wear hats or baseball caps
    You can't carry bundles on your head if you wear a hat
But I am not carrying a bundle
    When I find heaps and heaps of hats against a wall
    I am ready to bargain
    I try on three-one with a narrow pink string around the brim
The vendor teeth sparkling under his gray moustache
    Holds up a small broken mirror
    "Beautiful," he beams
    He knows how to persuade the Blanc, the foreign lady!
I move on under my straw hat with its pink trim
Suddenly I am in Haitian "supermarket"
    Heaps of mangos breadfruit watermelon tomatoes
    Bunches of bananas
    Flat baskets heaped with rice and flour
        and beans – red black speckled
        measured out with a cup or a tin can
    Salt in chunks sugar in bags baskets of spices
A boy comes by hawking fried plantain in a basket

continued

An old woman sitting beside a plastic bucket lifts
the ladle to show me it is molasses she offers
Then I see the children
Two of them – a boy of eight and his sister perhaps seven
Sitting behind the baskets of rice and beans with their mother
Listless eyes stare at the passing feet
And I remember
These children cannot go to school
their parents cannot pay

I hear a thin wail above the hum of voices
And again a persistent cry
My eyes follow the sound
Under a table of candles and soap
a baby lying on a blanket
on a mat
screammg
Mother is methodically piling up long bars of soap that have
toppled over

My eyes are wet remembering
I want to hold and comfort this child
Will she get to put on a red checked school shirt and hold
A tiny piece of chalk and write her name?
Will she wear red ribbons in her hair?

AGING IN PLACE

When I use

    A cane

People get out

    Of my way,

Open doors

    For me.

At first I

    Resented it -

I'm fine

    I'm fine.

Then I learned

    To accept

    To honor

Their good heartedness.

Because of my age

    A lot can pass me by

continued

I can hang on to what

    I love

And let the rest –

    The pop culture stuff

    Today's songs, movie stars

Pass me by – Unless

    One touches me –

A sound, a feeling,

    A voice, a face

But most of the time

    It's what I love

Have always loved –

    The trees, the birds,

The mountains,

    Children, Books

QUEEN ANNE'S LACE

The fields are white with lace.
    Looking closer - each lacy circle
Has a tiny black dot at its center.

When the fields are full of lace
    I always remember another summer.
We went from lovely lace to deep sorrow
    A plane was down in Boston.

One survivor
    Not my Dad
    Not my Mother.

Some comfort to know at least,
    Blows to their heads
Must have rendered them unconscious
    They didn't feel the flames.

One couple on the plane was found
    Holding hands.
I like to think it was them.

Years have passed
    Time has layered joys
On the time of lace.

A grandson born
    When those same fields
Were white with lace

A son married another summer
    A daughter also
So joys and sorrows
    Have come to me
In the season of Queen Anne's Lace.

CPSIA information can be obtained
at www.ICGtesting.com
Printed in the USA
FFHW01n1356160718
47408967-50600FF

9 781949 066067